P9-DFX-586

DATE DUE

MR 6 '07	MAR	SE 1 7 '14
	2. 6 - 00	
MR 1 z. '09	JAN X 8 2017	
AP 09 09		
MY 6 09		
MY 27 09		
JE 11 09		
90 /3 00		
	OCT 1 2 2017	

Demco No. 62-0549

GRAPHIC BIOGRAPHIES

MOLLY PITCHER

YOUNG AMERICAN PATRIOT

by Jason Glaser

C. 1

illustrated by Tod Smith, Bill Anderson,
and Charles Barnett III

Consultant:

Dr. David G. Martin

Author, *A Molly Pitcher Sourcebook*

Capstone
press

Mankato, Minnesota

Graphic Library is published by Capstone Press,
151 Good Counsel Drive, P.O. Box 669, Mankato, Minnesota 56002.
www.capstonepress.com

Printed in the United States of America

1 2 3 4 5 6 11 10 09 08 07 06

Library of Congress Cataloging-in-Publication Data
Glaser, Jason.
Molly Pitcher: young American patriot / by Jason Glaser; illustrated by Tod Smith, Bill Anderson, and Charles Barnett III.
p. cm.—(Graphic library. Graphic biographies)
Includes bibliographical references and index.
ISBN-13: 978-0-7368-5486-3 (hardcover)
ISBN-10: 0-7368-5486-X (hardcover)
1. Pitcher, Molly, 1754–1832—Juvenile literature. 2. Monmouth, Battle of, Freehold, N.J., 1778—Juvenile literature. 3. Women revolutionaries—United States—Biography—Juvenile literature. 4. Revolutionaries—United States—Biography—Juvenile literature. 5. United States—History—Revolution, 1775–1783—Biography—Juvenile literature. I. Smith, Tod, ill. II. Anderson, Bill, 1963– ill. III. Barnett, Charles, III, ill. IV. Title. V. Series.
E241.M7G58 2006
973.3'34092—dc22 2005032296

Summary: Describes the legend of Revolutionary War heroine Molly Pitcher in graphic novel format.

Art Direction and Design
Bob Lentz

Production Designer
Alison Thiele

Colorist
Melissa Kaercher

Editor
Angie Kaelberer

TABLE OF CONTENTS

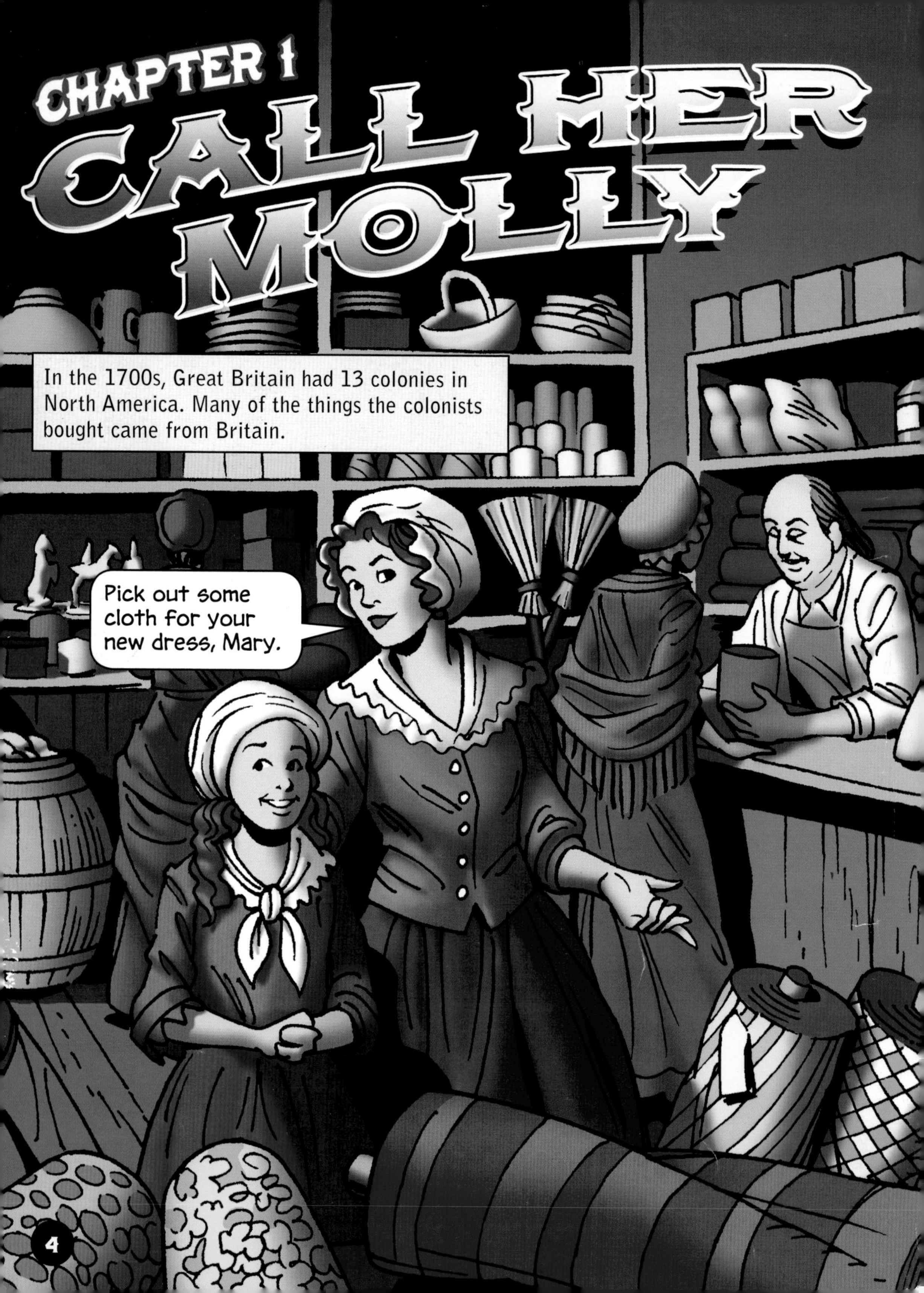
CHAPTER 1
CALL HER MOLLY
In the 1700s, Great Britain had 13 colonies in North America. Many of the things the colonists bought came from Britain.
Pick out some cloth for your new dress, Mary.

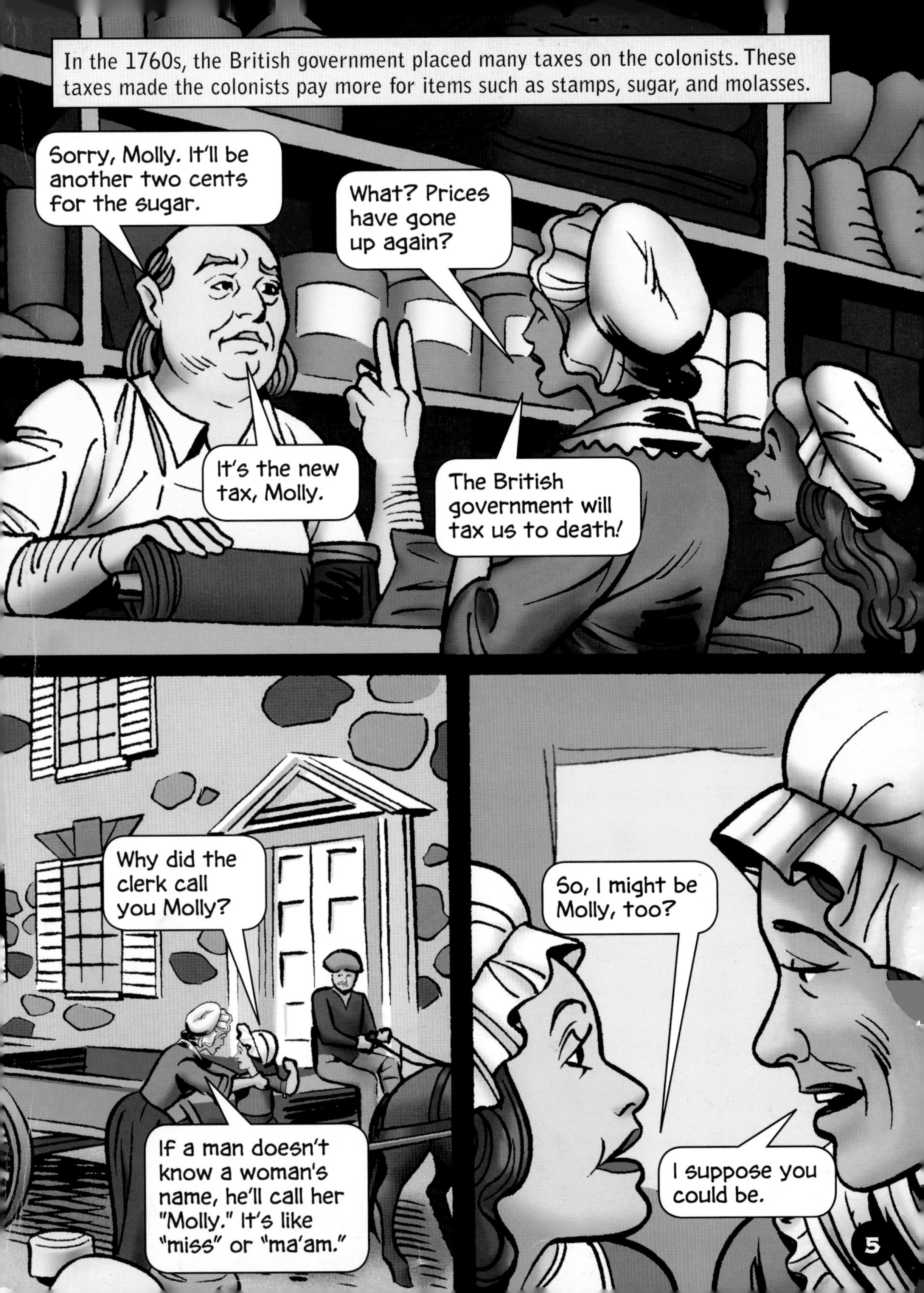
In the 1760s, the British government placed many taxes on the colonists. These taxes made the colonists pay more for items such as stamps, sugar, and molasses.
Sorry, Molly. It'll be another two cents for the sugar.
What? Prices have gone up again?
It's the new tax, Molly.
The British government will tax us to death!
Why did the clerk call you Molly?
If a man doesn't know a woman's name, he'll call her "Molly." It's like "miss" or "ma'am."
So, I might be Molly, too?
I suppose you could be.

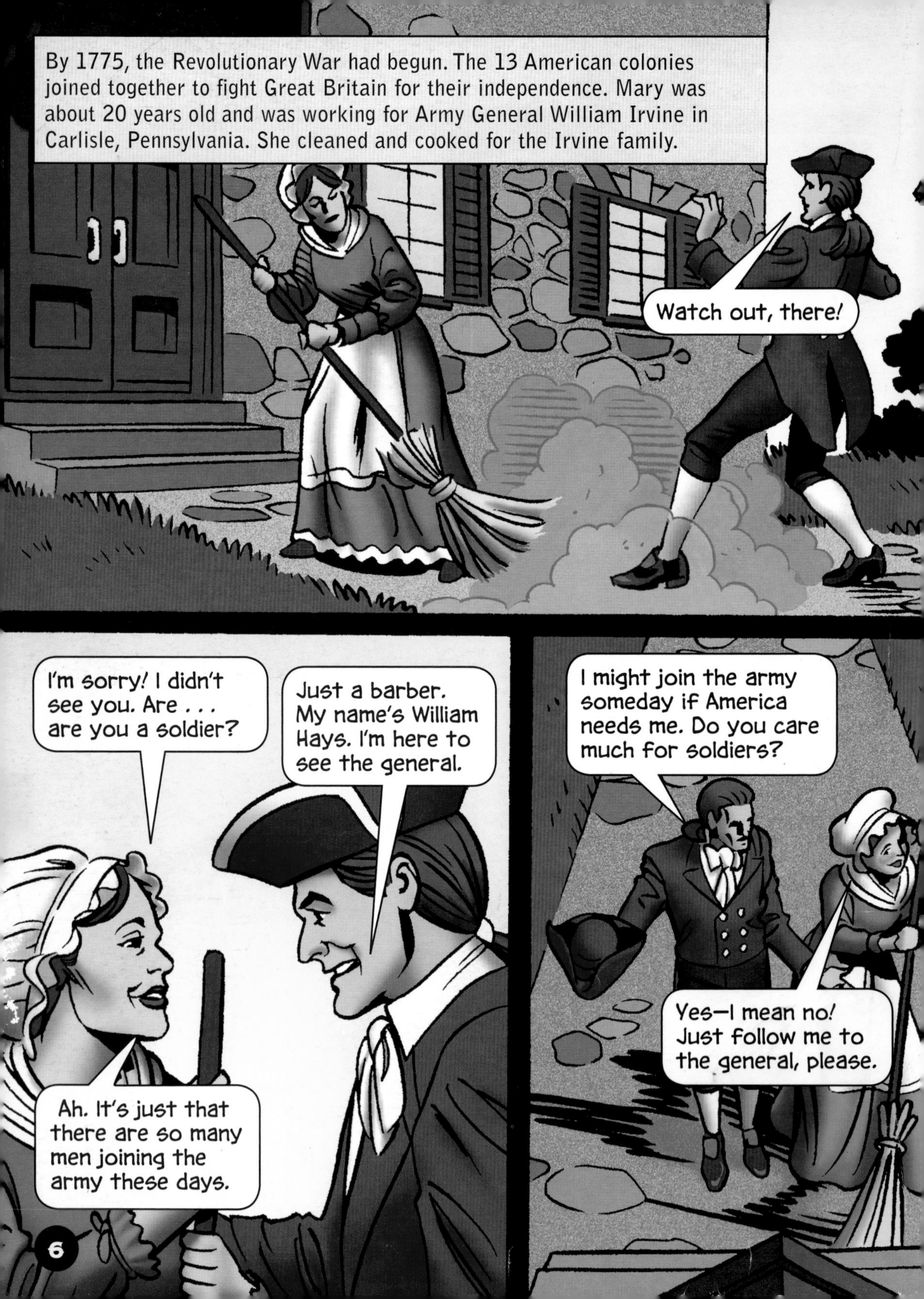
By 1775, the Revolutionary War had begun. The 13 American colonies joined together to fight Great Britain for their independence. Mary was about 20 years old and was working for Army General William Irvine in Carlisle, Pennsylvania. She cleaned and cooked for the Irvine family.
Watch out, there!
I'm sorry! I didn't see you. Are . . . are you a soldier?
Just a barber. My name's William Hays. I'm here to see the general.
Ah. It's just that there are so many men joining the army these days.
I might join the army someday if America needs me. Do you care much for soldiers?
Yes—I mean no! Just follow me to the general, please.

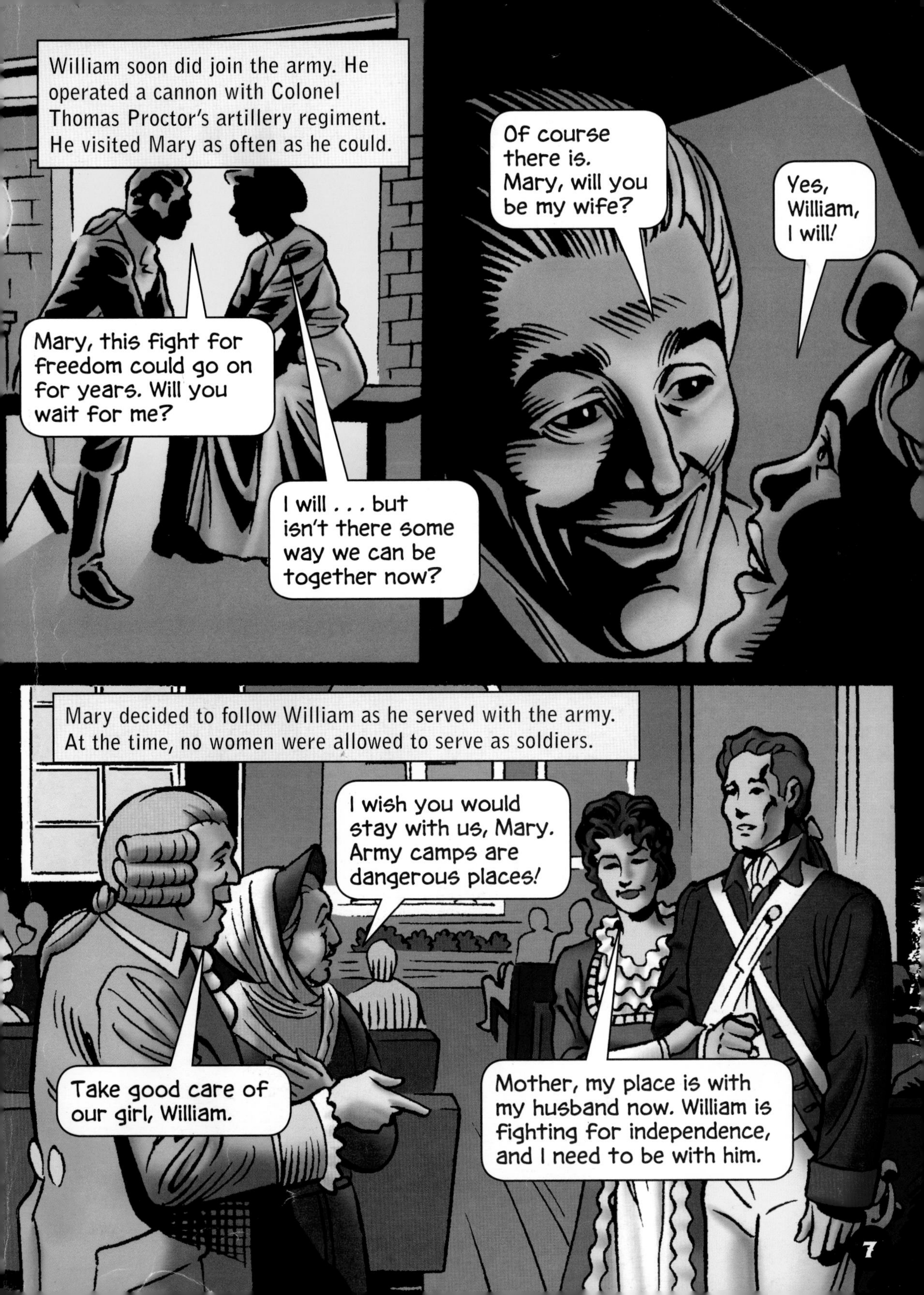
William soon did join the army. He operated a cannon with Colonel Thomas Proctor's artillery regiment. He visited Mary as often as he could.
Mary, this fight for freedom could go on for years. Will you wait for me?
I will . . . but isn't there some way we can be together now?
Of course there is. Mary, will you be my wife?
Yes, William, I will!
Mary decided to follow William as he served with the army. At the time, no women were allowed to serve as soldiers.
I wish you would stay with us, Mary. Army camps are dangerous places!
Take good care of our girl, William.
Mother, my place is with my husband now. William is fighting for independence, and I need to be with him.

CHAPTER 2
FOLLOWING THE ARMY

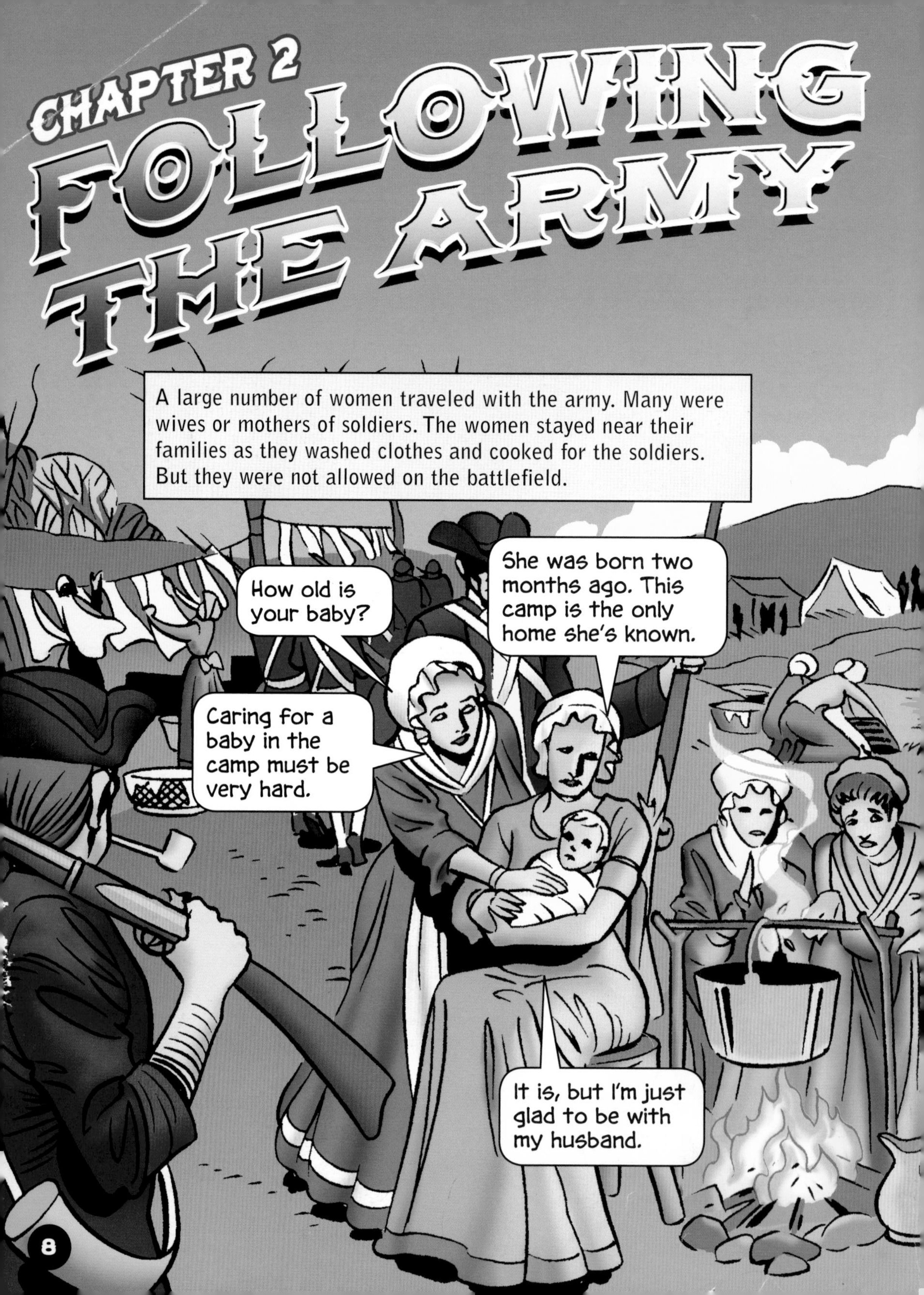
A large number of women traveled with the army. Many were wives or mothers of soldiers. The women stayed near their families as they washed clothes and cooked for the soldiers. But they were not allowed on the battlefield.
How old is your baby?
She was born two months ago. This camp is the only home she's known.
Caring for a baby in the camp must be very hard.
It is, but I'm just glad to be with my husband.

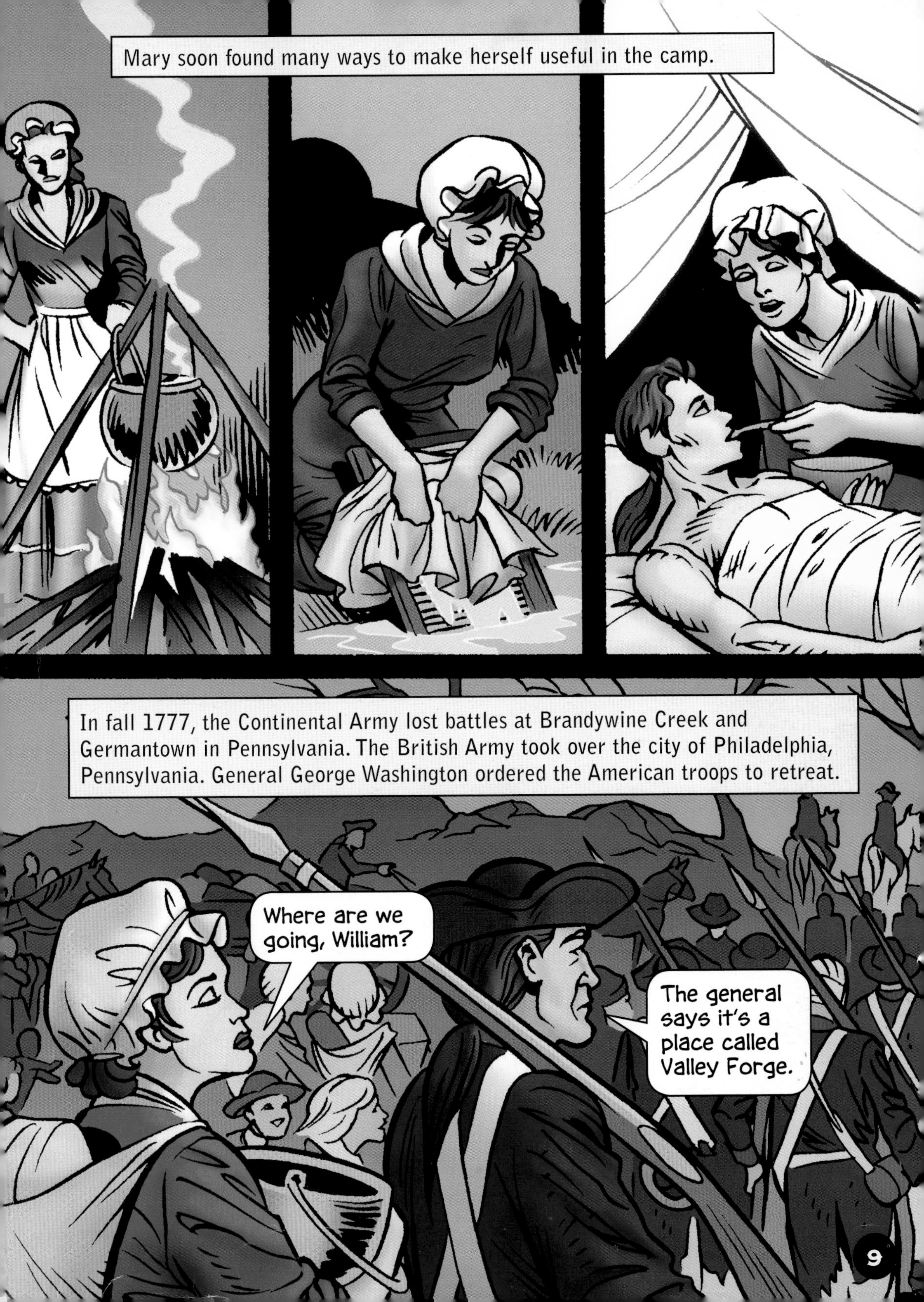
Mary soon found many ways to make herself useful in the camp.
In fall 1777, the Continental Army lost battles at Brandywine Creek and Germantown in Pennsylvania. The British Army took over the city of Philadelphia, Pennsylvania. General George Washington ordered the American troops to retreat.
Where are we going, William?
The general says it's a place called Valley Forge.

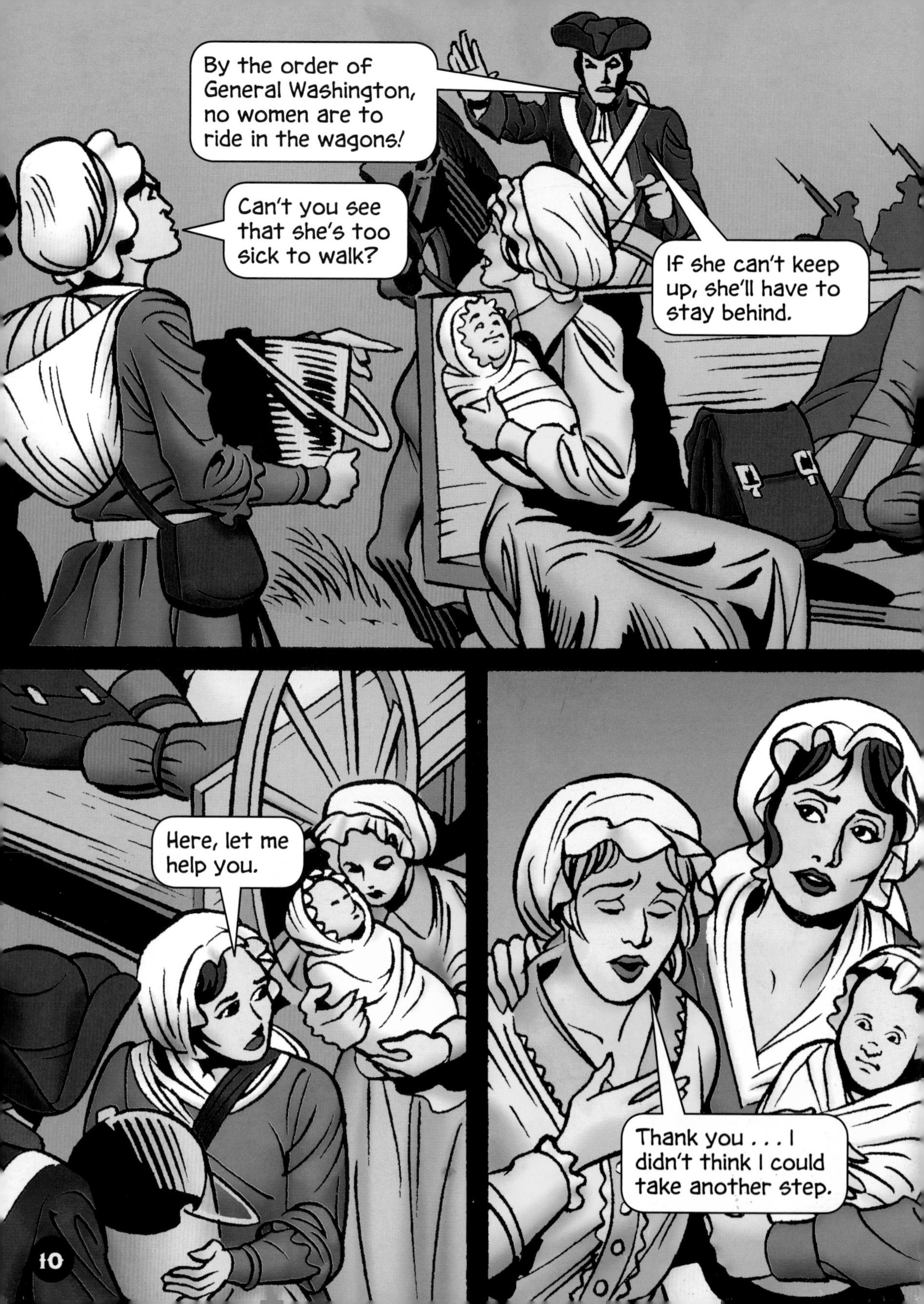
By the order of General Washington, no women are to ride in the wagons!
Can't you see that she's too sick to walk?
If she can't keep up, she'll have to stay behind.
Here, let me help you.
Thank you . . . I didn't think I could take another step.

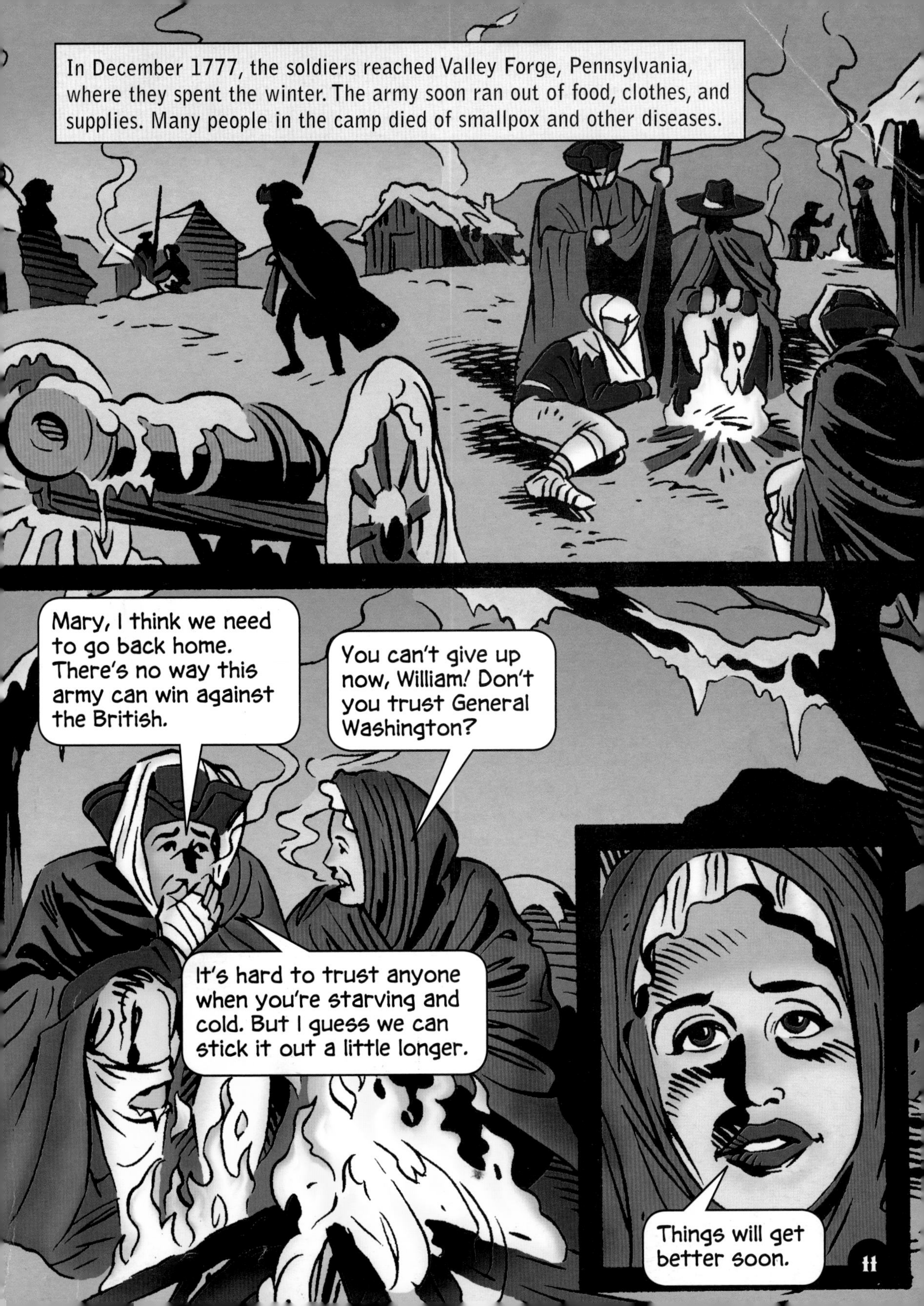
In December 1777, the soldiers reached Valley Forge, Pennsylvania, where they spent the winter. The army soon ran out of food, clothes, and supplies. Many people in the camp died of smallpox and other diseases.
Mary, I think we need to go back home. There's no way this army can win against the British.
You can't give up now, William! Don't you trust General Washington?
It's hard to trust anyone when you're starving and cold. But I guess we can stick it out a little longer.
Things will get better soon.

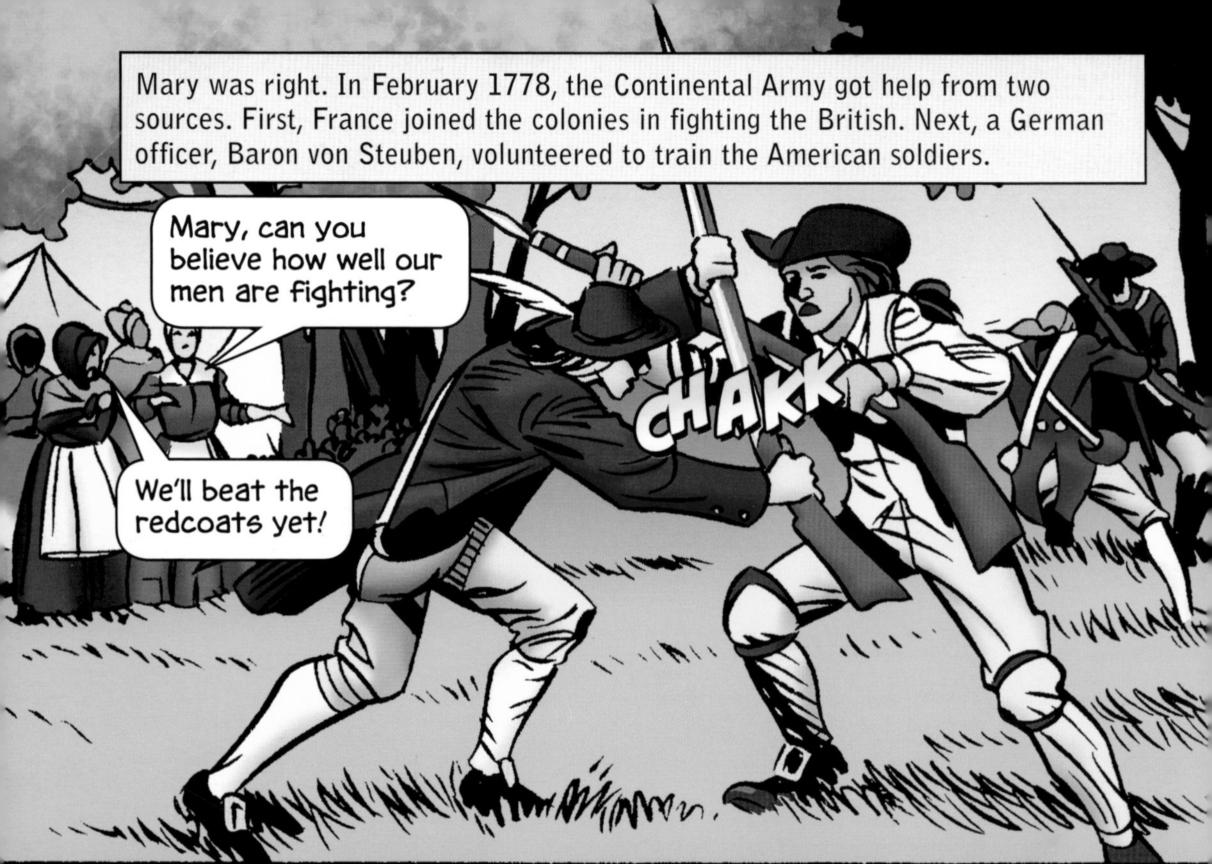
Mary was right. In February 1778, the Continental Army got help from two sources. First, France joined the colonies in fighting the British. Next, a German officer, Baron von Steuben, volunteered to train the American soldiers.
Mary, can you believe how well our men are fighting?
We'll beat the redcoats yet!
CHAKK

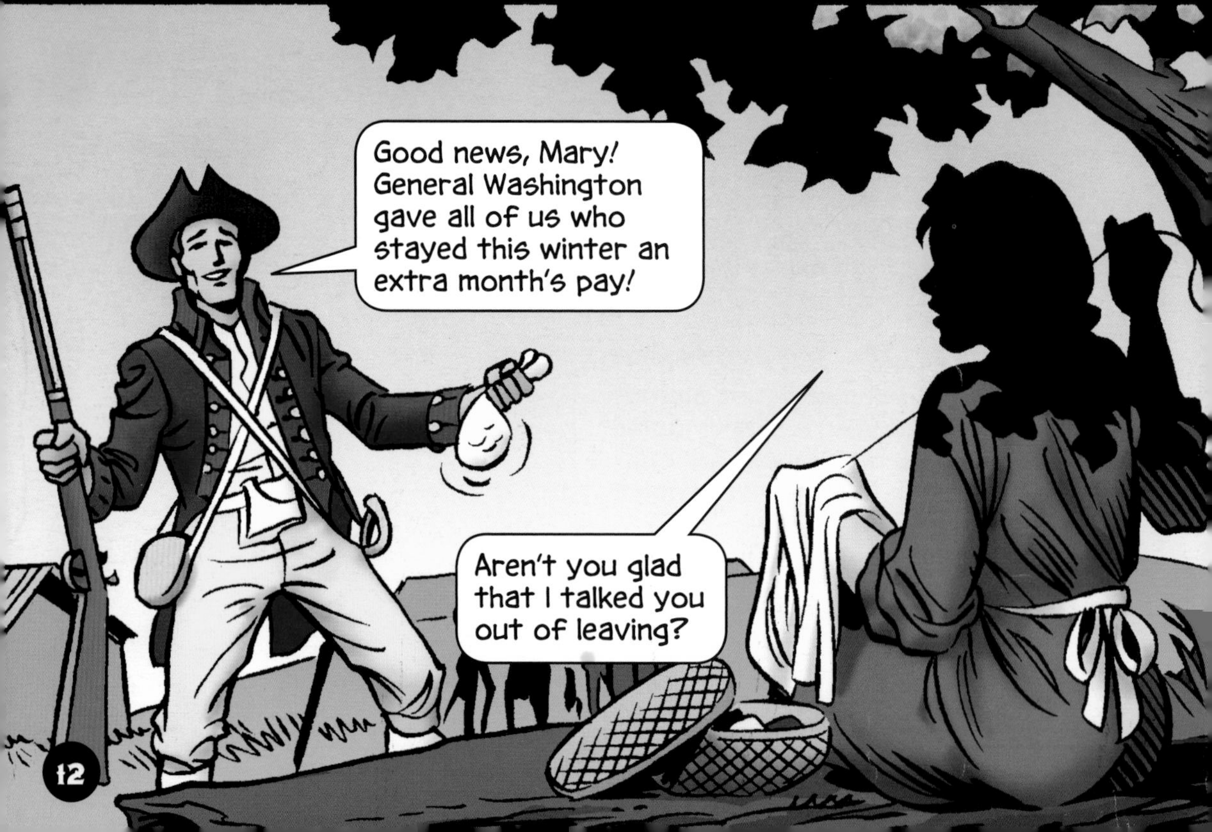
Good news, Mary! General Washington gave all of us who stayed this winter an extra month's pay!
Aren't you glad that I talked you out of leaving?

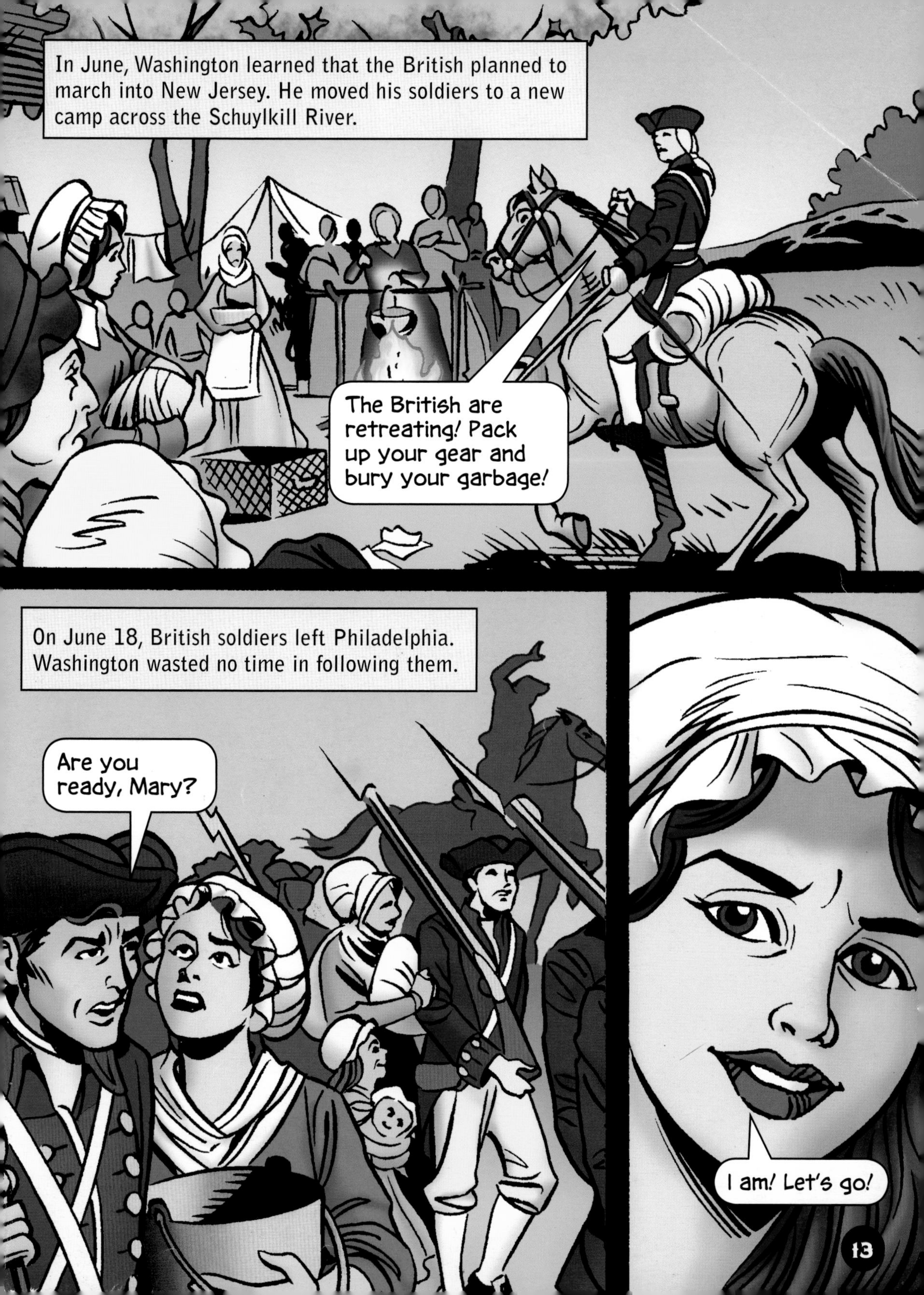
In June, Washington learned that the British planned to march into New Jersey. He moved his soldiers to a new camp across the Schuylkill River.
The British are retreating! Pack up your gear and bury your garbage!
On June 18, British soldiers left Philadelphia. Washington wasted no time in following them.
Are you ready, Mary?
I am! Let's go!

CHAPTER 3
BRAVERY IN BATTLE

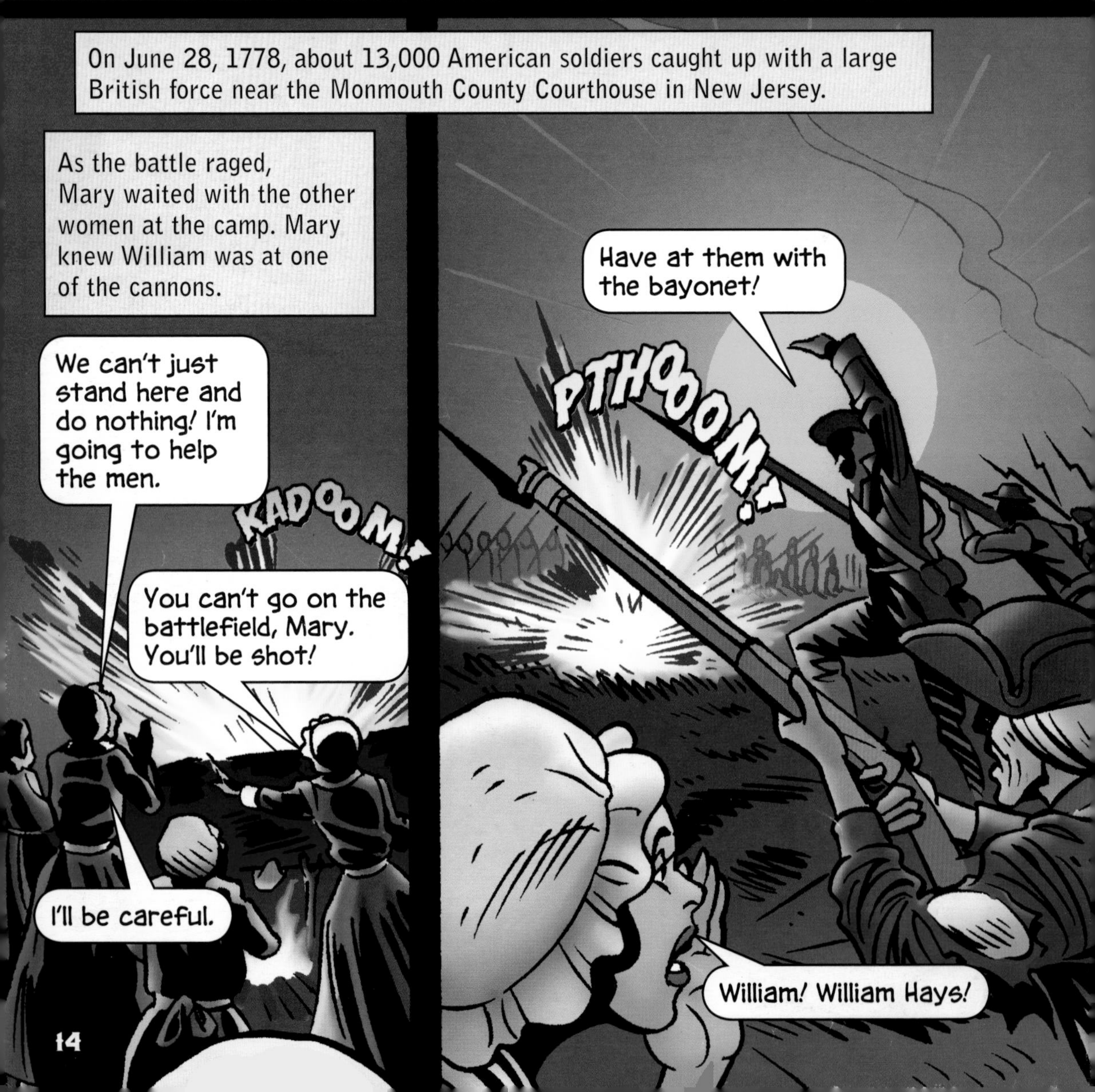
On June 28, 1778, about 13,000 American soldiers caught up with a large British force near the Monmouth County Courthouse in New Jersey.
As the battle raged, Mary waited with the other women at the camp. Mary knew William was at one of the cannons.
We can't just stand here and do nothing! I'm going to help the men.
KADOOM!
You can't go on the battlefield, Mary. You'll be shot!
I'll be careful.
Have at them with the bayonet!
PTHOOOM!
William! William Hays!

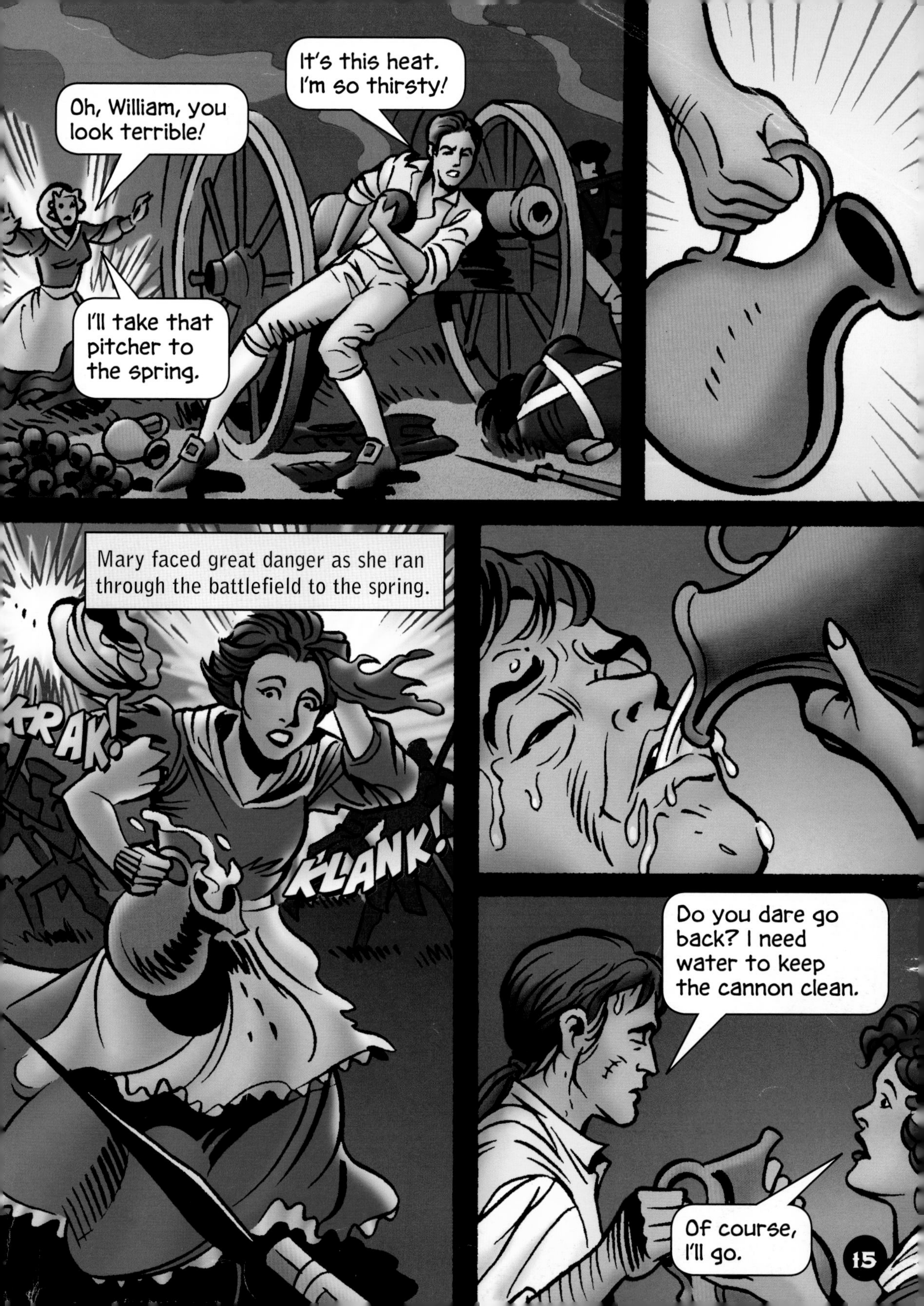
Oh, William, you look terrible!
It's this heat. I'm so thirsty!
I'll take that pitcher to the spring.
Mary faced great danger as she ran through the battlefield to the spring.
KRAK!
KLANK!
Do you dare go back? I need water to keep the cannon clean.
Of course, I'll go.

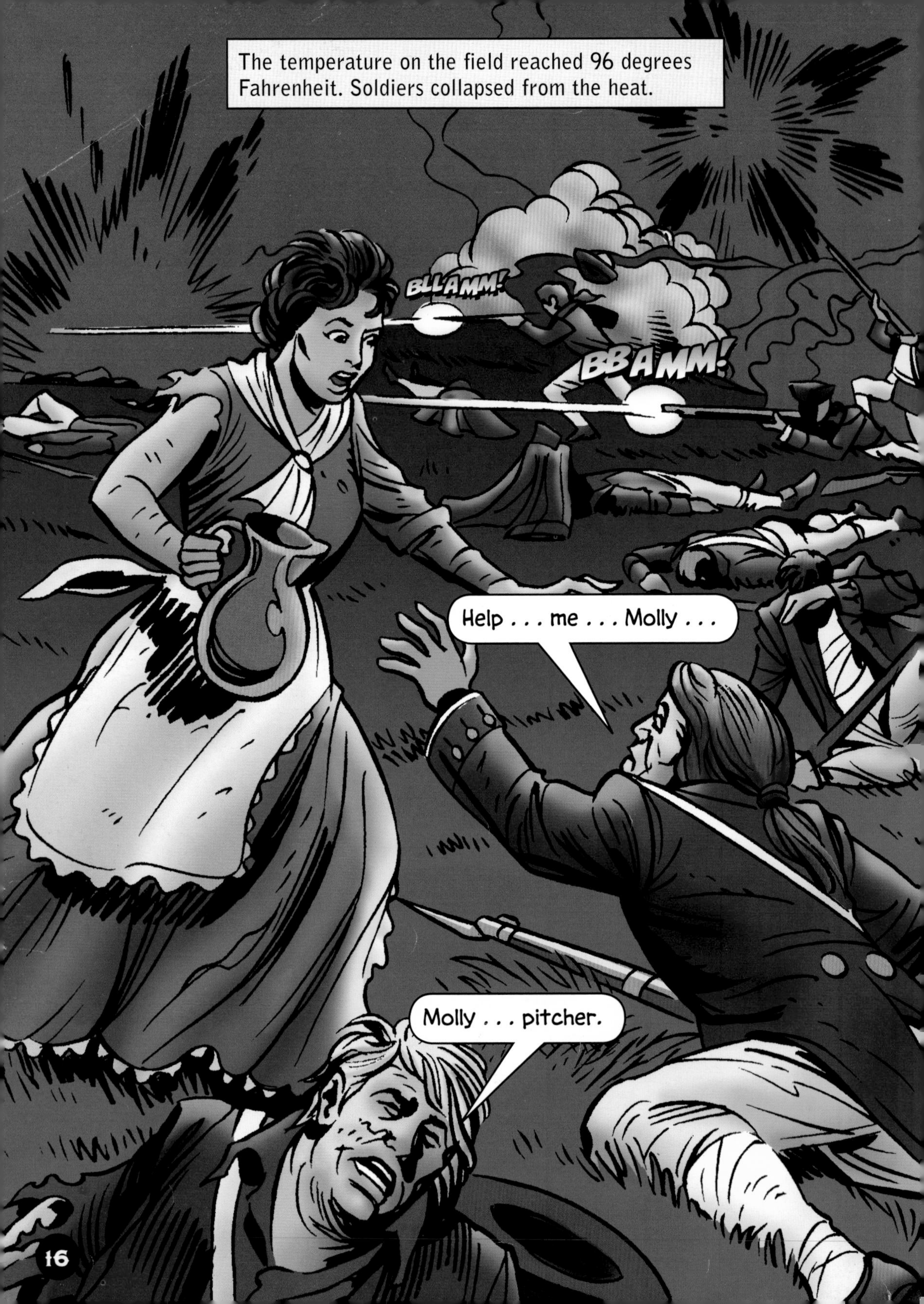

The temperature on the field reached 96 degrees Fahrenheit. Soldiers collapsed from the heat.
BLLAMM!
BBAMM!
Help . . . me . . . Molly . . .
Molly . . . pitcher.

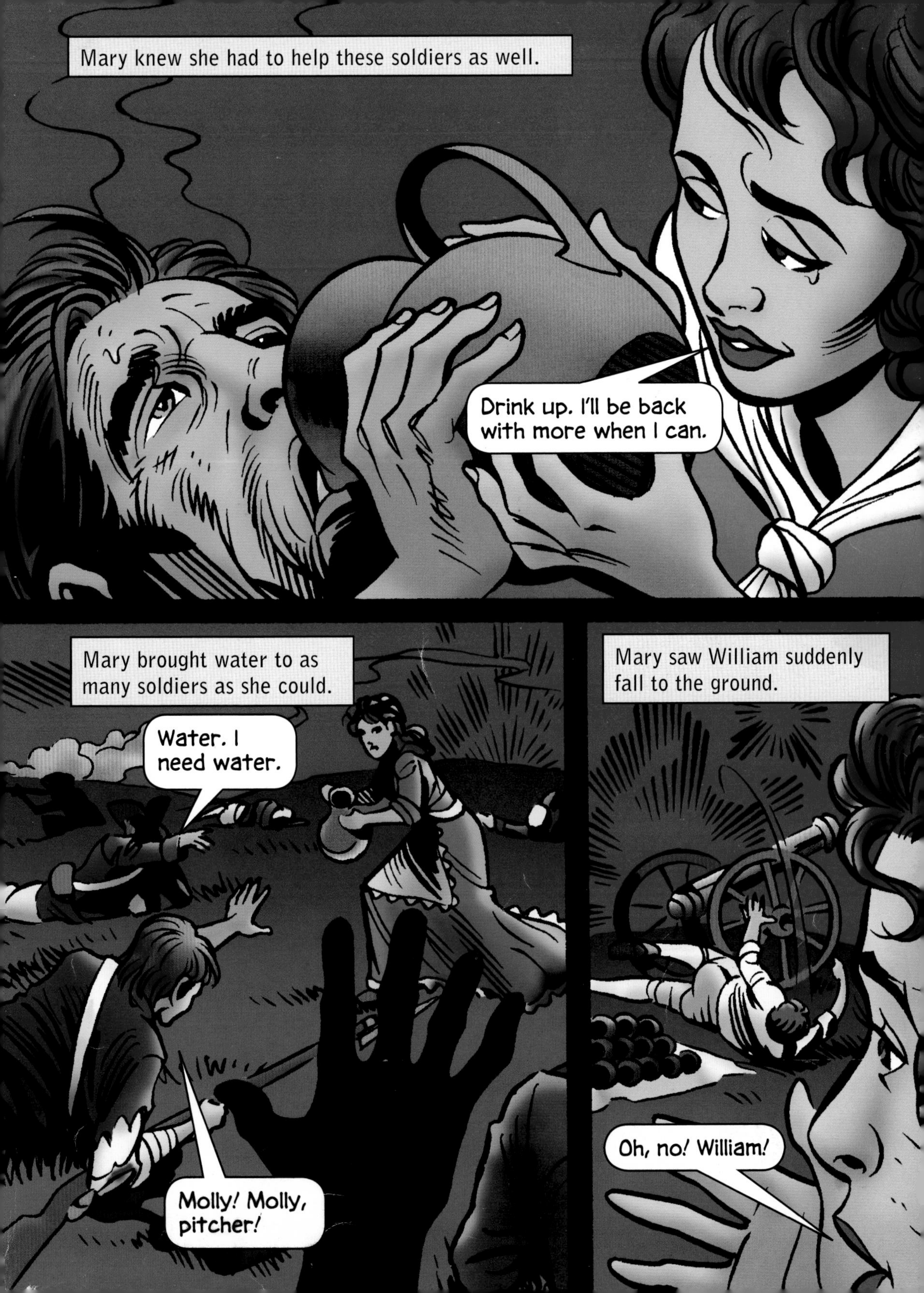
Mary knew she had to help these soldiers as well.
Drink up. I'll be back with more when I can.
Mary brought water to as many soldiers as she could.
Water. I need water.
Molly! Molly, pitcher!
Mary saw William suddenly fall to the ground.
Oh, no! William!

Lie here and rest. Save your strength.

Mary . . .

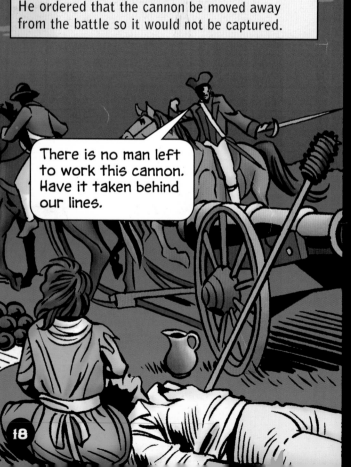

An American officer saw that William was hurt. He ordered that the cannon be moved away from the battle so it would not be captured.

There is no man left to work this cannon. Have it taken behind our lines.

Who says a man must fire the cannon?

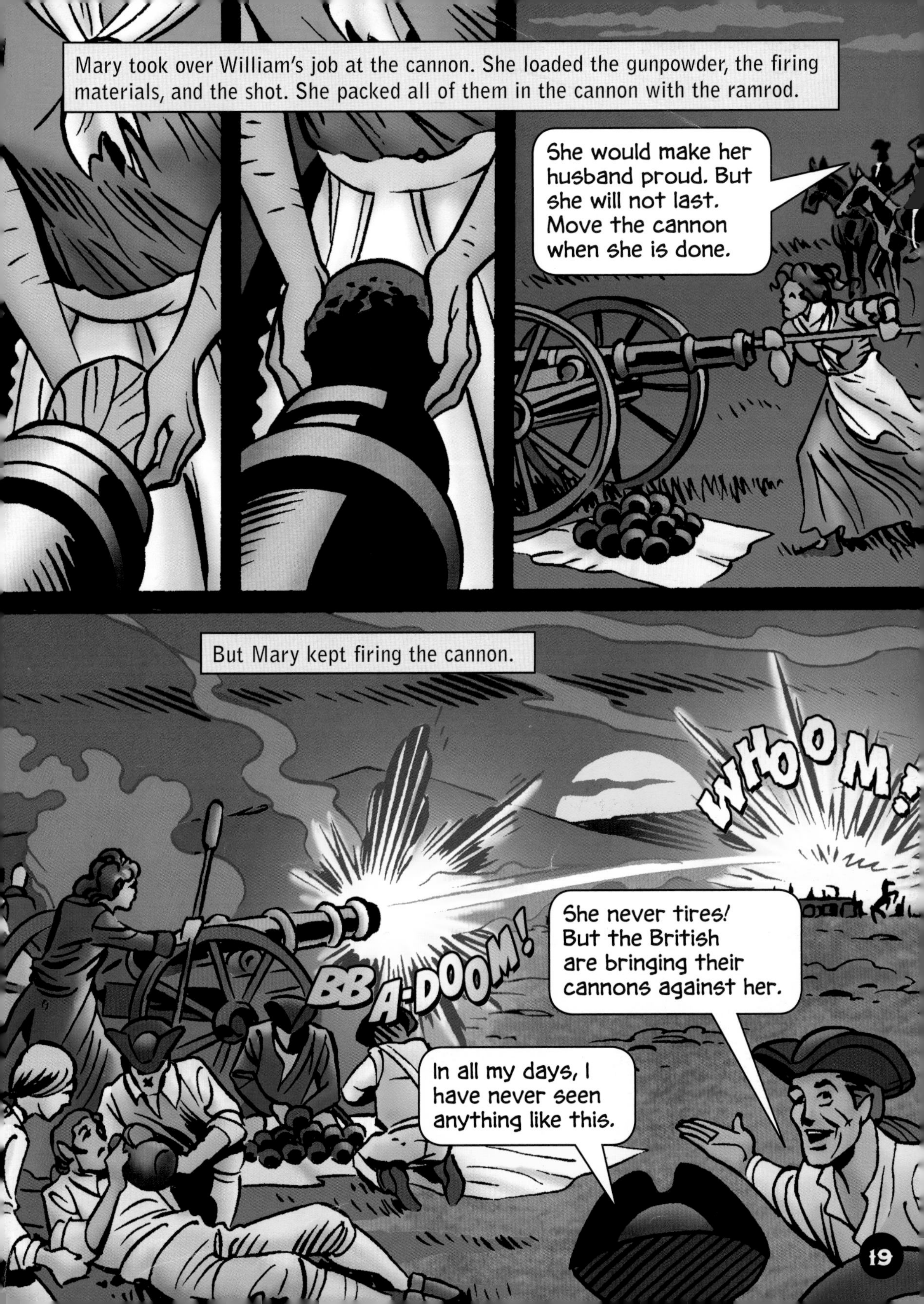
Mary took over William's job at the cannon. She loaded the gunpowder, the firing materials, and the shot. She packed all of them in the cannon with the ramrod.
She would make her husband proud. But she will not last. Move the cannon when she is done.
But Mary kept firing the cannon.
WHOOM!
BB A-DOOM!
She never tires! But the British are bringing their cannons against her.
In all my days, I have never seen anything like this.

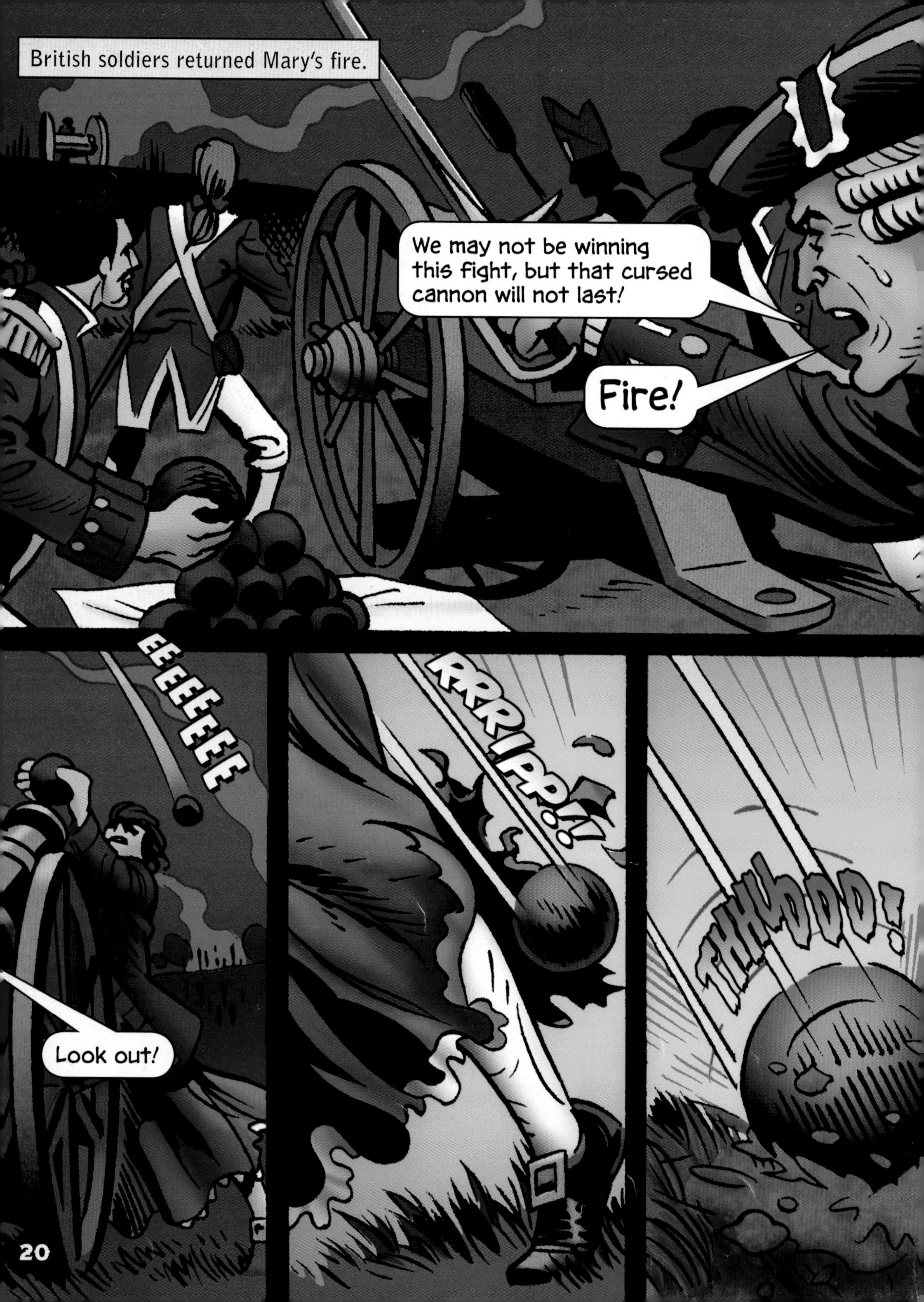
British soldiers returned Mary's fire.
We may not be winning this fight, but that cursed cannon will not last!
Fire!
EEEEEEEEE
Look out!
RRRIPP!!
THUDDD!

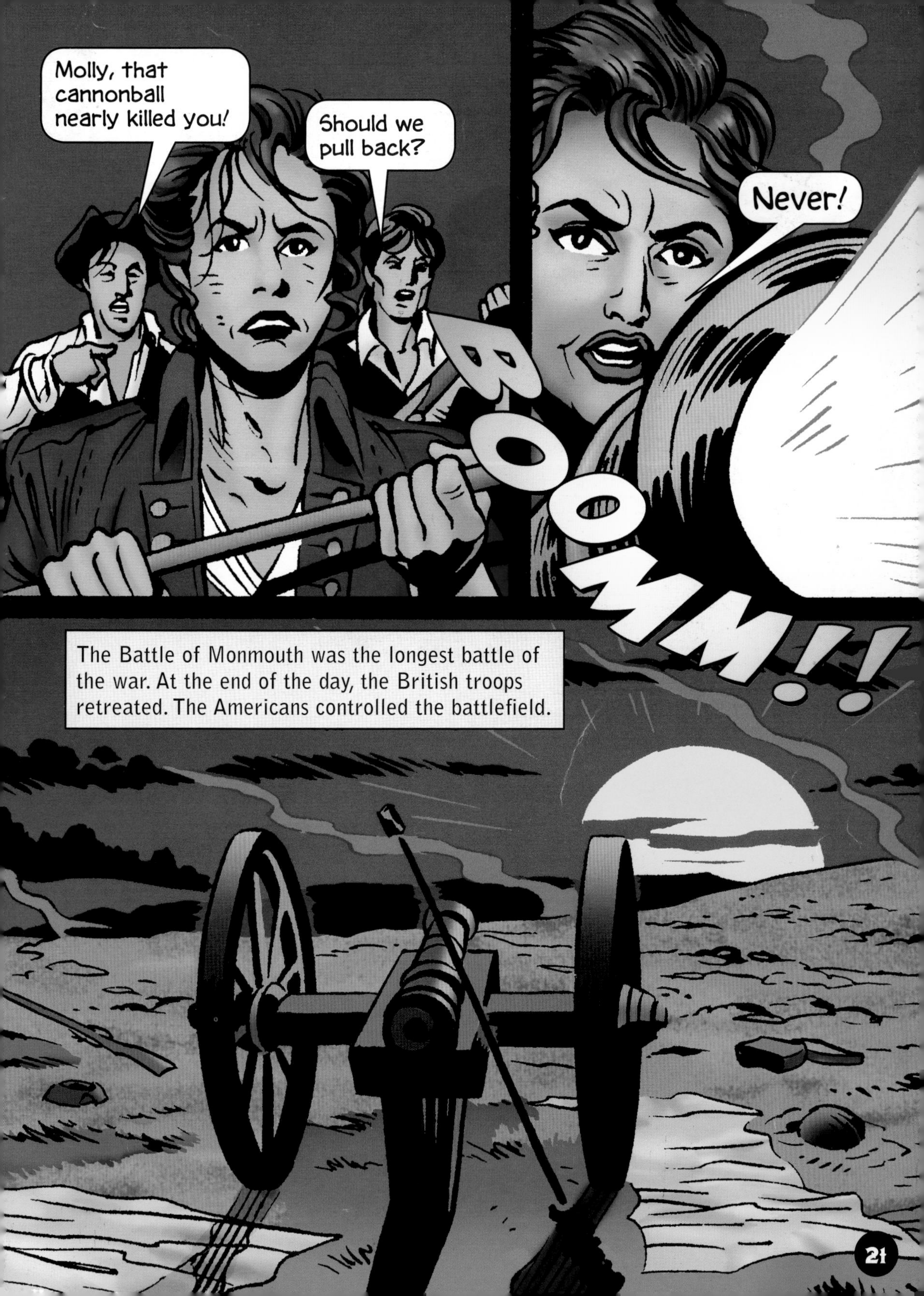
Molly, that cannonball nearly killed you!
Should we pull back?
Never!
BOOOMM!!!
The Battle of Monmouth was the longest battle of the war. At the end of the day, the British troops retreated. The Americans controlled the battlefield.

CHAPTER 4
HEROINE OF THE REVOLUTION

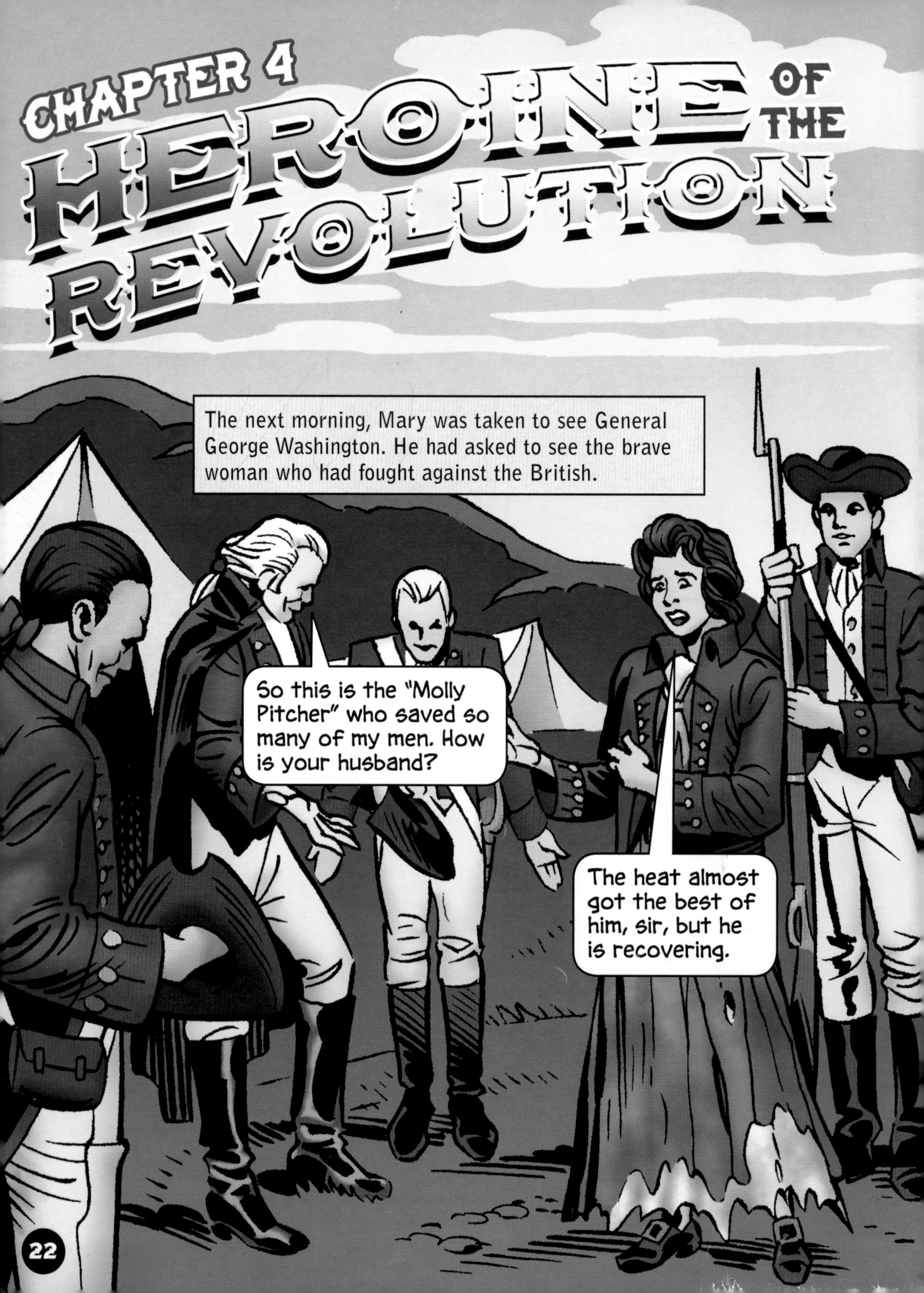
The next morning, Mary was taken to see General George Washington. He had asked to see the brave woman who had fought against the British.
So this is the "Molly Pitcher" who saved so many of my men. How is your husband?
The heat almost got the best of him, sir, but he is recovering.

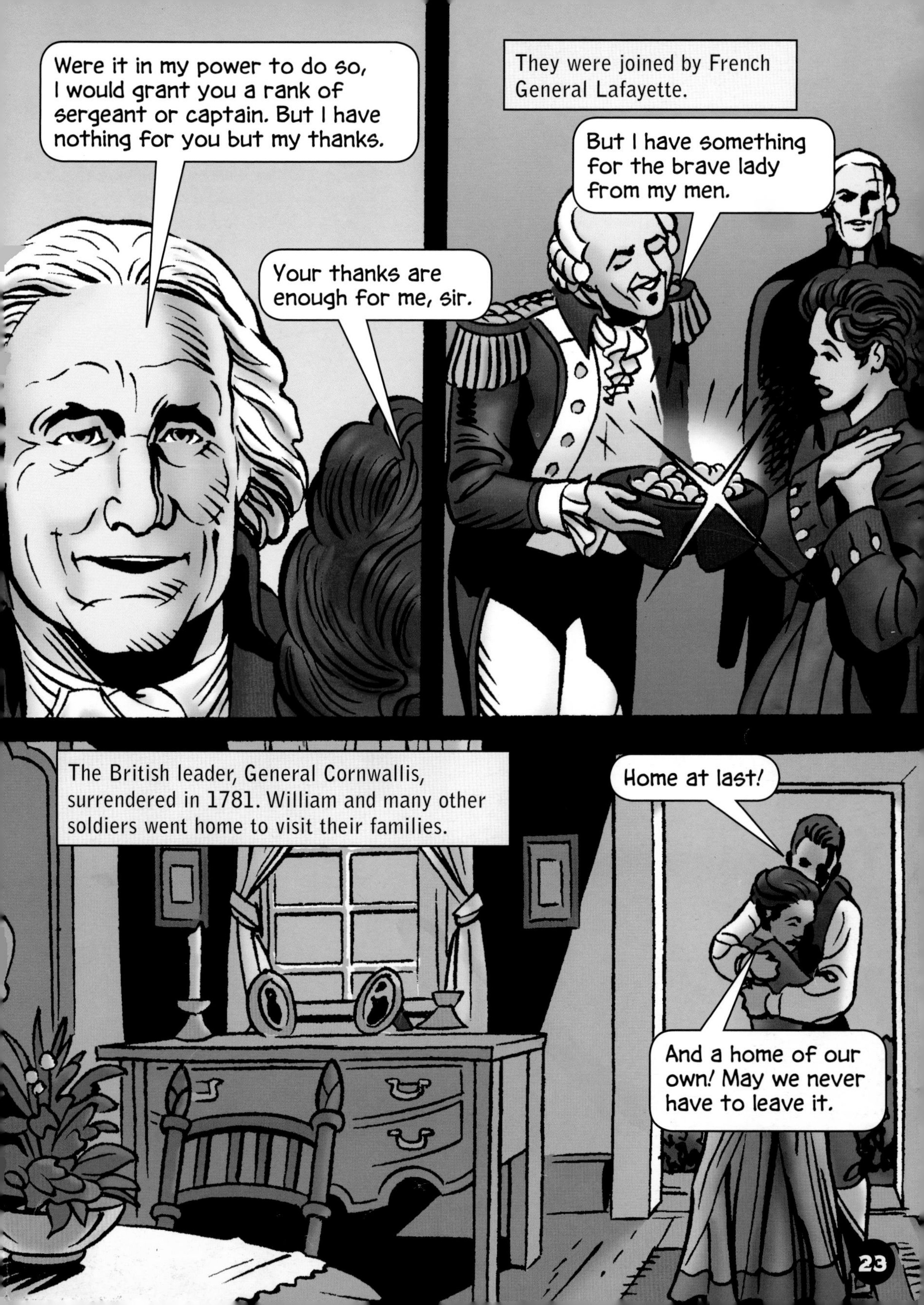
Were it in my power to do so, I would grant you a rank of sergeant or captain. But I have nothing for you but my thanks.
Your thanks are enough for me, sir.
They were joined by French General Lafayette.
But I have something for the brave lady from my men.
The British leader, General Cornwallis, surrendered in 1781. William and many other soldiers went home to visit their families.
Home at last!
And a home of our own! May we never have to leave it.

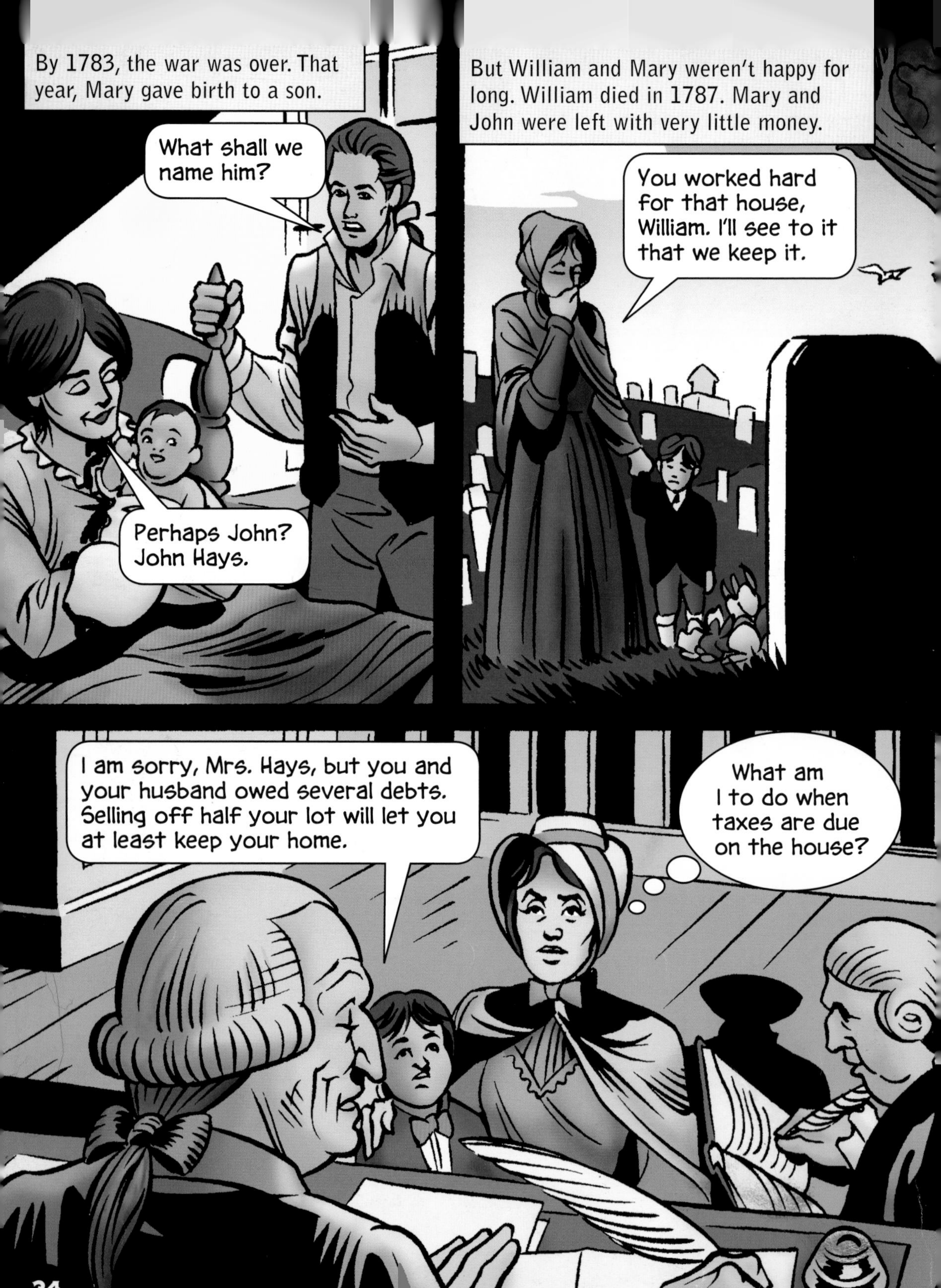
By 1783, the war was over. That year, Mary gave birth to a son.
What shall we name him?
Perhaps John? John Hays.
But William and Mary weren't happy for long. William died in 1787. Mary and John were left with very little money.
You worked hard for that house, William. I'll see to it that we keep it.
I am sorry, Mrs. Hays, but you and your husband owed several debts. Selling off half your lot will let you at least keep your home.
What am I to do when taxes are due on the house?

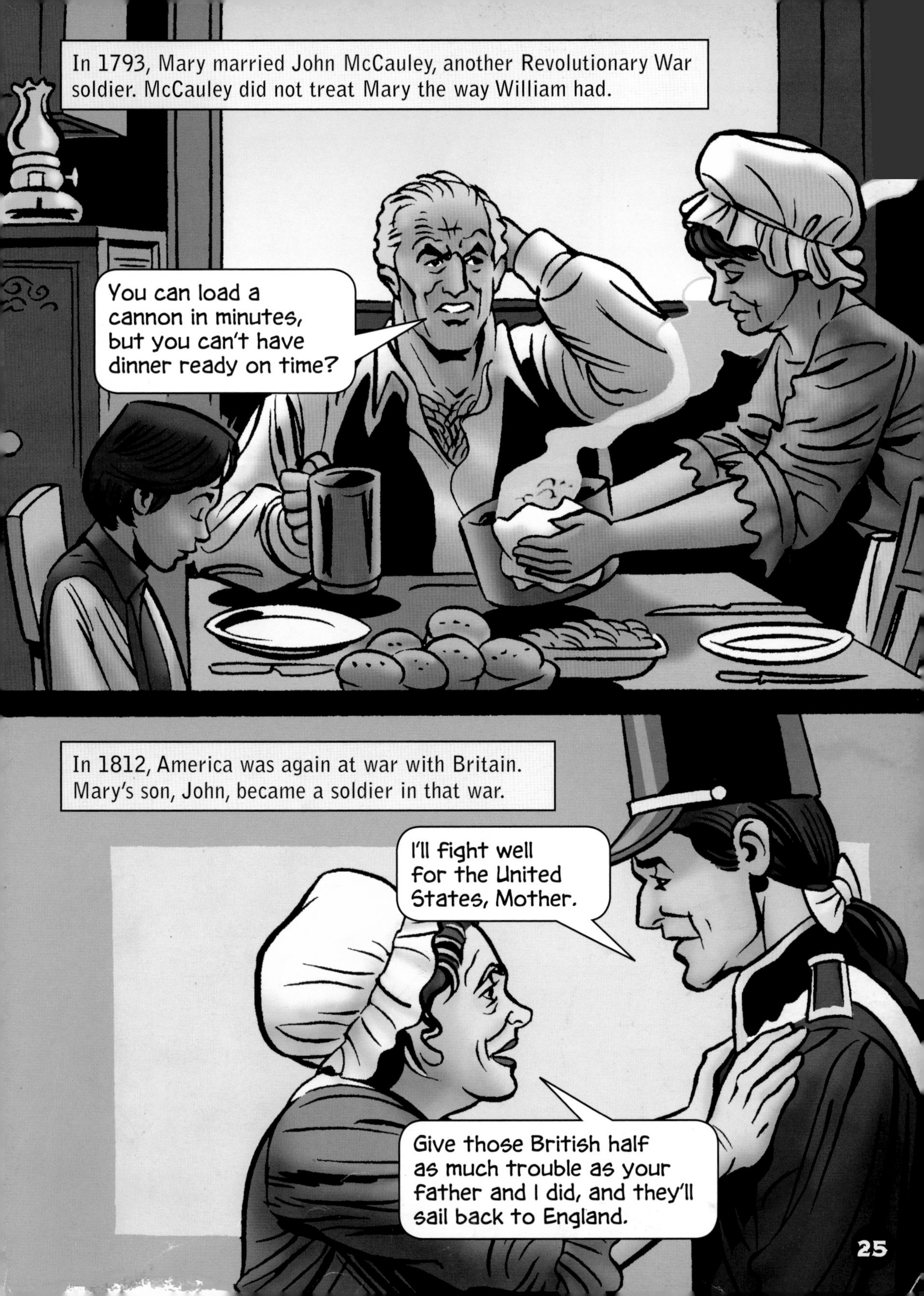
In 1793, Mary married John McCauley, another Revolutionary War soldier. McCauley did not treat Mary the way William had.
You can load a cannon in minutes, but you can't have dinner ready on time?
In 1812, America was again at war with Britain. Mary's son, John, became a soldier in that war.
I'll fight well for the United States, Mother.
Give those British half as much trouble as your father and I did, and they'll sail back to England.

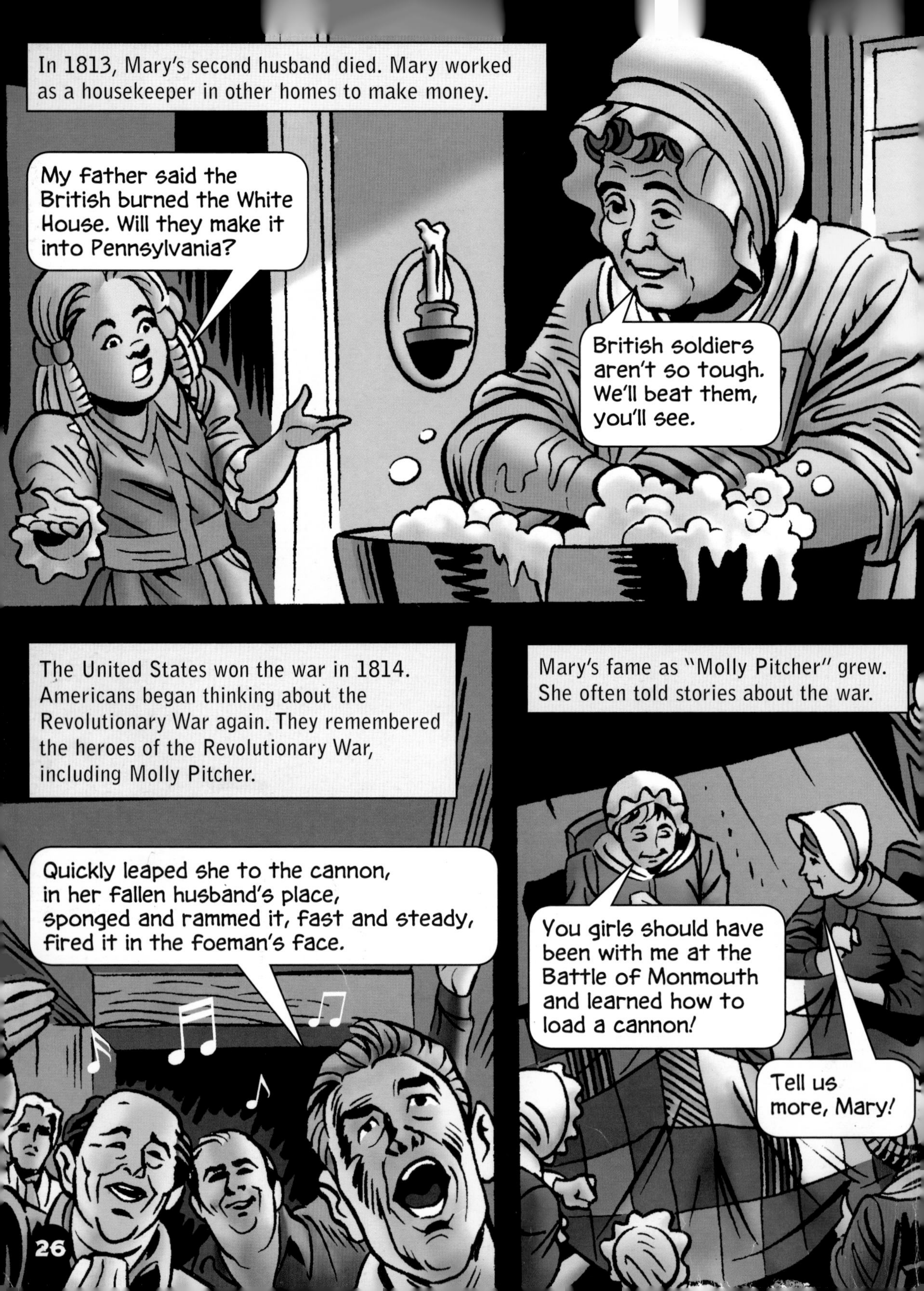
In 1813, Mary's second husband died. Mary worked as a housekeeper in other homes to make money.
My father said the British burned the White House. Will they make it into Pennsylvania?
British soldiers aren't so tough. We'll beat them, you'll see.
The United States won the war in 1814. Americans began thinking about the Revolutionary War again. They remembered the heroes of the Revolutionary War, including Molly Pitcher.
Quickly leaped she to the cannon, in her fallen husband's place, sponged and rammed it, fast and steady, fired it in the foeman's face.
Mary's fame as "Molly Pitcher" grew. She often told stories about the war.
You girls should have been with me at the Battle of Monmouth and learned how to load a cannon!
Tell us more, Mary!

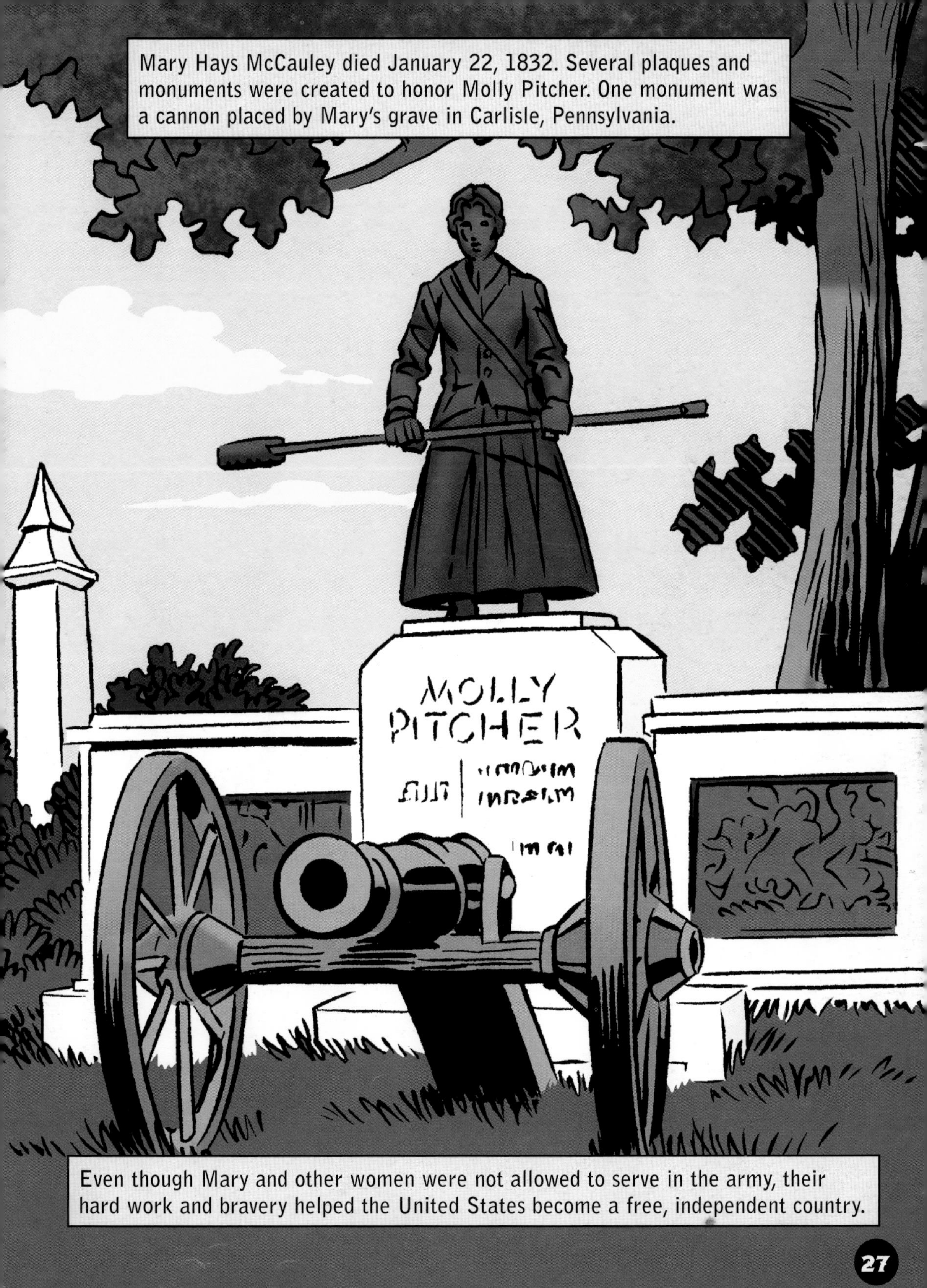
Mary Hays McCauley died January 22, 1832. Several plaques and monuments were created to honor Molly Pitcher. One monument was a cannon placed by Mary's grave in Carlisle, Pennsylvania.
MOLLY PITCHER
Even though Mary and other women were not allowed to serve in the army, their hard work and bravery helped the United States become a free, independent country.

MORE ABOUT MOLLY PITCHER

Mary Hays McCauley was a real person, but she is not the only person credited with being Molly Pitcher. Historians do not know Molly Pitcher's birth name, her husband's name, or anything about her for certain. People believe Mary may have been Molly Pitcher because she used to talk about being in the Revolutionary War and the Battle of Monmouth.

The legend of Molly Pitcher has come to represent all the women who fought bravely during the Revolutionary War. Margaret Corbin fought at the battle of Fort Washington. She also fired her husband's cannon and received a pension. Sally St. Clair, Deborah Sampson, and a woman who called herself Samuel Gay dressed as men to fight in the Revolutionary War. These women's stories were mixed with Molly Pitcher's legend over time.

Some historians believe there may have been hundreds or even thousands of women at Revolutionary War battlefields. The women collected rifles and ammunition from the battlefields and brought water for cannons. These women may also have helped create the Molly Pitcher legend.

In 1822, Mary received a yearly pension of $40 from the state of Pennsylvania. Only two other women received government pensions for their role in the Revolutionary War.

 Mary's last name was misspelled as "McKolly" on one of the monuments built in her honor. The monument also lists her first name as "Mollie" instead of "Mary."

 After the Revolutionary War, people wrote songs about Molly Pitcher. In some of them, she was referred to as "Captain Molly."

 Molly Pitcher sometimes appears in paintings wearing men's clothes. Soldiers said Molly Pitcher put on an army jacket and other men's clothing to fight.

 An average cannonball used in the Revolutionary War weighed 6 pounds (2.7 kilograms).

 So many cannonballs were fired at Monmouth that people still find them buried in the ground there.

GLOSSARY

bayonet (BAY-uh-net)—a long metal blade attached to the end of a rifle

colony (KAHL-uh-nee)—a settlement in a distant land that is ruled by another country

general (JEN-ur-uhl)—an army officer of the highest rank

independence (in-di-PEN-duhnss)—freedom from the control of other people or things

legend (LEJ-uhnd)—a story handed down from earlier times

revolution (rev-uh-LOO-shun)—an uprising by the people of a country that attempts to change its system of government

INTERNET SITES

FactHound offers a safe, fun way to find Internet sites related to this book. All of the sites on FactHound have been researched by our staff.

Here's how:

1. *Visit www.facthound.com*
2. Type in this special code **073685486X** for age-appropriate sites. Or enter a search word related to this book for a more general search.
3. Click on the **Fetch It** button.

FactHound will fetch the best sites for you!

READ MORE

Brimner, Larry Dane. *Molly Pitcher.* Tall Tales. Minneapolis: Compass Point Books, 2004.

Rockwell, Anne F. *They Called Her Molly Pitcher.* New York: Knopf, 2002.

Ruffin, Frances E. *Molly Pitcher.* American Legends. New York: PowerKids Press, 2002.

BIBLIOGRAPHY

Blumenthal, Walter Hart. *Women Camp Followers of the American Revolution.* New York: Arno Press, 1974.

Bohrer, Melissa Lukeman. *Glory, Passion, and Principle: The Story of Eight Remarkable Women at the Core of the American Revolution.* New York: Atria Books, 2003.

Carrington, Henry B. *Battles of the American Revolution.* New York: The New York Times, 1968.

Gundersen, Joan R. *To Be Useful to the World: Women in Revolutionary America, 1740–1790.* New York: Twayne Publishers, 1996.

Martin, David G. *A Molly Pitcher Sourcebook.* Hightstown, N.J.: Longstreet House, 2003.

INDEX